Assessing the Role of K-12 Academic Standards in States

WORKSHOP SUMMARY

Alexandra Beatty, *Rapporteur*

Committee on State Standards in Education:
A Workshop Series

Center for Education

Division of Behavioral and Social Sciences and Education

NATIONAL RESEARCH COUNCIL
OF THE NATIONAL ACADEMIES

THE NATIONAL ACADEMIES PRESS
Washington, D.C.
www.nap.edu

THE NATIONAL ACADEMIES PRESS 500 Fifth Street, N.W. Washington, DC 20001

NOTICE: The project that is the subject of this report was approved by the Governing Board of the National Research Council, whose members are drawn from the councils of the National Academy of Sciences, the National Academy of Engineering, and the Institute of Medicine. The members of the committee responsible for the report were chosen for their special competences and with regard for appropriate balance.

This study was supported by a contract between the National Academy of Sciences and the James B. Hunt, Jr. Institute for Educational Leadership and Policy. Any opinions, findings, conclusions, or recommendations expressed in this publication are those of the author(s) and do not necessarily reflect the views of the organizations or agencies that provided support for the project.

International Standard Book Number-13: 978-0-309-12035-7
International Standard Book Number-10: 0-309-12035-7

Additional copies of this report are available from National Academies Press, 500 Fifth Street, N.W., Lockbox 285, Washington, DC 20055; (800) 624-6242 or (202) 334-3313 (in the Washington metropolitan area); Internet, http://www.nap.edu.

Printed in the United States of America

Suggested citation: National Research Council. (2008). *Assessing the Role of K-12 Academic Standards in States: Workshop Summary*. Alexandra Beatty, Rapporteur. Committee on State Standards in Education: A Workshop Series. Center for Education, Division of Behavioral and Social Sciences and Education. Washington, DC: The National Academies Press.

THE NATIONAL ACADEMIES

Advisers to the Nation on Science, Engineering, and Medicine

The **National Academy of Sciences** is a private, nonprofit, self-perpetuating society of distinguished scholars engaged in scientific and engineering research, dedicated to the furtherance of science and technology and to their use for the general welfare. Upon the authority of the charter granted to it by the Congress in 1863, the Academy has a mandate that requires it to advise the federal government on scientific and technical matters. Dr. Ralph J. Cicerone is president of the National Academy of Sciences.

The **National Academy of Engineering** was established in 1964, under the charter of the National Academy of Sciences, as a parallel organization of outstanding engineers. It is autonomous in its administration and in the selection of its members, sharing with the National Academy of Sciences the responsibility for advising the federal government. The National Academy of Engineering also sponsors engineering programs aimed at meeting national needs, encourages education and research, and recognizes the superior achievements of engineers. Dr. Charles M. Vest is president of the National Academy of Engineering.

The **Institute of Medicine** was established in 1970 by the National Academy of Sciences to secure the services of eminent members of appropriate professions in the examination of policy matters pertaining to the health of the public. The Institute acts under the responsibility given to the National Academy of Sciences by its congressional charter to be an adviser to the federal government and, upon its own initiative, to identify issues of medical care, research, and education. Dr. Harvey V. Fineberg is president of the Institute of Medicine.

The **National Research Council** was organized by the National Academy of Sciences in 1916 to associate the broad community of science and technology with the Academy's purposes of furthering knowledge and advising the federal government. Functioning in accordance with general policies determined by the Academy, the Council has become the principal operating agency of both the National Academy of Sciences and the National Academy of Engineering in providing services to the government, the public, and the scientific and engineering communities. The Council is administered jointly by both Academies and the Institute of Medicine. Dr. Ralph J. Cicerone and Dr. Charles M. Vest are chair and vice chair, respectively, of the National Research Council.

www.national-academies.org

COMMITTEE ON STATE STANDARDS IN EDUCATION: A WORKSHOP SERIES

LORRAINE MCDONNELL (*Chair*), Department of Political Science, University of California at Santa Barbara
THOMAS B. CORCORAN, Consortium for Policy Research and Education, Teacher's College, Columbia University
ROBERT LINN, Department of Education (emeritus), University of Colorado
WILLIAM TATE, Department of Arts and Sciences, Washington University in St. Louis
LAURESS WISE, Human Resources Research Organization, Monterey, CA
KAREN WIXSON, School of Education, University of Michigan

Staff

STUART ELLIOTT, Co-Study Director
LISA TOWNE, Co-Study Director
ALEXANDRA BEATTY, Senior Program Officer
MARGARET HILTON, Senior Program Officer
KELLY DUNCAN, Program Assistant

Preface

Every state in the United States, the District of Columbia, and the Department of Defense Education Activity now has its own academic standards, at least in core subjects. These documents vary in their structure, level of specificity, and other characteristics. Professional societies have also developed standards, in mathematics, English language arts, science, social studies, civics, foreign languages, and other academic subjects, and many states have drawn on these as they prepared their own standards documents. Other organizations have also offered standards and benchmarks. For example, the Mid-continent Research for Education and Learning (McREL) offers standards developed with the goal of applying a consistent structure and degree of rigor and specificity to standards in diverse subjects (see http://www.mcrel.org/standards-benchmarks/ [April 2008]).

This abundance of standards reflects a vigorous response to the call for high standards articulated in the National Commission on Excellence in Education's 1983 report *A Nation at Risk*, and it also poses a variety of questions for educators, policy makers, and the public. What role are these standards playing? What are the strengths and weaknesses of the reform efforts that have been anchored by these standards? How are these standards applied, and how might standards-based reforms be improved? Would a move toward national standards in core academic subjects lead to improved instruction and learning? Would it be feasible?

The National Research Council (NRC), with support from the James B. Hunt, Jr. Institute for Educational Leadership and Policy (Hunt Institute), is sponsoring a set of workshops to examine questions about common and state-specific standards. The Hunt Institute asked the NRC to organize these workshops for the purpose of providing research-based information about the way standards are currently working and the possible advantages and disadvantages of alternative approaches. These workshops were planned by the Committee on State Standards in Education, whose membership reflected diverse policy and research perspectives on the issues. This report summarizes the presentations and discussions from the first workshop, held in January 2008, which focused on the current role of standards in the states. As a workshop summary, this report does not reflect the conclusions or judgments of the steering committee, but rather describes the research and perspectives that were presented.

The committee identified three components to the charge for the first workshop: a review of the policy and research context in which current standards-based reform efforts are operating, a consideration of how the costs of standards and accountability systems might be calculated, and an analysis of similarities and differences among states' content and performance standards. (The second workshop, held in March 2008, addressed possible options for establishing common education standards and the tradeoffs that this course might entail.)

This workshop summary has been reviewed in draft form by individuals chosen for their diverse perspectives and technical expertise, in accordance with procedures approved by the Report Review Committee of the NRC. The purpose of this independent review is to provide candid and critical comments that will assist the institution in making its published report as sound as possible and to ensure that the report meets institutional standards for objectivity, evidence, and responsiveness to the charge. The review comments and draft manuscript remain confidential to protect the integrity of the process. We thank the following individuals for their review of this report: Martha Darling, consultant, Ann Arbor, MI; Michael W. Kirst, School of Education, Stanford University; Peter McWalters, Elementary and Secondary Education, Rhode Island Department of Education; and Barbara Reys, Learning Teaching and Curriculum, University of Missouri. Although the reviewers listed above provided many constructive comments and suggestions, they were not asked to endorse the content of the report nor did they see the final draft of the report before its release. The review of this report was overseen by Diana C. Pullin, School of Education, Boston College. Appointed by the NRC, she was responsible for making certain that an independent examination of this report was carried out in accordance with institutional procedures and that all review comments were carefully considered. Responsibility for the final content of this report rests entirely with the author and the institution.

The committee would also like to thank the co-study directors for this project, Stuart Elliott and Lisa Towne, for their leadership throughout; Margaret Hilton for her help in planning and organizing the workshop; Alix Beatty for drafting the report; and Kelly Duncan for excellent logistical support. We also gratefully acknowledge the contributions of report editor Genie Grohman and report review officer Kirsten Sampson-Snyder. Last, but not least, the committee extends sincere thanks to Judith Rizzo and her colleagues at the Hunt Institute for their support and advice throughout the process.

Lorraine McDonnell, *Chair*
Committee on State Standards in Education:
A Workshop Series

Contents

1

Policy Context

The position that there should be a single set of academic standards in core subjects that states would be encouraged or required to adopt or closely model is not new, but a number of groups have recently advocated it. The discussion surrounding renewal of the No Child Left Behind Act (NCLB) has focused new attention on the effects of the current model, in which states adopt widely differing standards. As Judith Rizzo of the James B. Hunt, Jr. Institute for Educational Leadership and Policy noted, in explaining the impetus for the workshop series, NCLB has shined a "spotlight on the incredible variability of state test scores, both within and among states."

Several groups, including the Commission on No Child Left Behind, the Education Trust, the Fordham Foundation, and the American Federation of Teachers, have argued in favor of voluntary national, or common, standards as a means of improving both achievement and equity (Goertz, 2007; Massell, 2008). Yet others have argued against common standards on the grounds that states, school districts, and teachers need flexibility to serve their students' needs and that reaching consensus on the shape and content of common standards—and even on a workable process for establishing that consensus—would be a formidable challenge. Complicating the discussion is the fact that evaluations of existing state standards in core subjects by such groups as Editorial Projects in Education, the Fordham Foundation, and the American Federation of Teachers have found many of them wanting (Editorial Projects in Education, 2008; Gross et al., 2005; American Federation of Teachers, 2003).

It should be noted that the general term "standards" is somewhat imprecise. In the context of the workshop it was generally used to refer to both content standards, which describe material that students should be expected to learn, and performance standards, which describe the level of proficiency or mastery expected of students. Most state standards specify both.

To support analysis of the conflicting points of view, the committee identified four questions to guide discussion:

1. What are the major roles that standards play in state K-12 education policy and practice?
2. What are the major strengths and weaknesses of K-12 state standards-based reform efforts with respect to achieving efficiency, equity, and quality? What are states doing to achieve these goals?
3. How and to what degree are the strengths and weaknesses of reform efforts related to the standards themselves? How and to what degree have the standards changed other education policies in states?
4. How and to what degree are the strengths and weaknesses of reform efforts related to having unique state standards?

For the first session of the workshop, the starting point was a presentation by Diane Massell (2008) on a series of interviews with education policy makers in five states: California, Florida, Massachusetts, North Dakota, and Texas.

VIEW FROM THE STATES

The purpose of Massell's interviews was to solicit opinions from a range of experienced policy makers who have been engaged in standards-based education reform, the catch all term for measures that states have taken to improve instruction and learning by organizing both policy and practice around clear, measurable standards. Massell and her colleagues hoped to trace both common themes and insights and possible differences, and to flag views that may be developing in response to current events. The five states were chosen to reflect both geographical diversity and diversity of experience with standards. California, which initiated its standards approach during the 1980s, was an early adopter, for example, while North Dakota adopted standards in response to federal requirements in 1994. The 21 interview subjects included officials or education aides from governors' offices, members of state boards of education, state legislators, and state education agency officials.

Massell began by highlighting the current, unprecedented degree of public engagement in the specifics of implementing standards-based systems, particularly the attention focused on the curriculum and instruction that make them concrete. She described standards-based reform as having had the effect of "opening Pandora's box" because it resulted in a new transparency with regard to curriculum and instruction. Massell was borrowing a phrase from a 1950s report that described districts as reluctant to allow the public to involve itself with potentially divisive questions about what and how children should be taught.

Although the minimum competency movement of the 1970s —as well as lawsuits in a number of states intended to force states to equalize school funding—brought increased focus on schools' accountability to states with regard to what students actually learned, the achievement bar was set relatively low. The standards-based reform movement that developed in response to *A Nation at Risk* (National Commission on Excellence in Education, 1983) expanded the role of standards, with a focus on rigorous requirements for high school graduation. As both national organizations, such as the National Council of Teachers of Mathematics, and individual states began to put forward more detailed statements of what students should be expected to know and be able to do, the concept of systemic reform, suggested by Smith and O'Day (1991), sharpened the focus on how standards might lead to the desired learning. The logic of systemic reform was that the primary elements of an educational system—such as curriculum, instruction, teacher preparation, professional development, and assessment—must all be aligned to carefully developed content and performance standards in order for those standards to affect teaching and learning. In this view, educators would still retain significant flexibility in meeting expectations but be held accountable for the results.

In 1994 the reauthorization of the Elementary and Secondary Education Act made standards-based reform the official national approach to public schooling by requiring states to set challenging standards aligned to assessments and accountability measures (Massell, 2008). The testing requirements imposed by NCLB in 2001 built on that commitment, requiring states to (1) publish challenging academic content standards in English/language arts and mathematics for each of grades 3 through 8 and one secondary grade, as well as standards for science in three grades, and (2) assess students in these grades and subjects annually and hold schools accountable for the results (http://www.ed.gov/policy/elsec/leg/esea02/index.html [April 2008]). Those requirements, and the consequences imposed by the law for failing to meet them have meant that parents and others have a significantly increased interest in the precise content of standards, curriculum, the tests used to measure proficiency, and the material covered in classrooms.

Massell's work found intense differences of opinion related to standards. Her interview subjects reported disagreement about how rigorous academic and performance standards are and should be, about whether measures that sharpen accountability also lead to an unacceptable narrowing of the curriculum, and about the fairness of accountability sanctions.

Yet despite tension around a number of issues, Massell noted that the leaders she and her colleagues interviewed generally take standards-based reform and accountability for granted, viewing this approach as a "central framework guiding state education policy and practice." Even the leaders from North Dakota, where standards were adopted largely under federal duress, viewed this approach as a part of the landscape that is not likely to change. The other four states had made a stronger commitment to standards, and the leaders from those states described them in such terms as "even more central over time" and "integral" to policy initiatives. Massell said that opening issues related to curriculum and instruction to public discussion has not had the effect of killing reform, as some may have feared, and the result has been "a surprising degree of agreement regarding the meaning and purpose of education."

The North Dakota respondents were more muted than the others, however. They were less likely to see standards as "central" to policy and tended to describe the effects of standards on classroom practice as marginal. Moreover, respondents from all five states reported that the focus on standards remains variable across and within both states and districts, as do their effects on instruction and learning.

Massell explained that the interviewers asked state education leaders for their impressions regarding several aspects of standards based reform, such as its impact on practice, learning opportunities, the quality of education, and resources. The leaders' responses to these issues generated an array of reactions from workshop discussants and participants.

EQUITY

The effects of standards-based accountability systems on achievement gaps and equality of opportunity for disadvantaged students was the first specific topic discussed in the interviews. In general, Massell reported, the state leaders believe that standards based reform has led to:

- greater awareness of and attention to the academic performance of disadvantaged students;
- the expectation that all students will meet rigorous standards;
- reductions in achievement gaps;
- a more uniform educational system (within states); and
- instruction that is tailored to the needs of individual students.

They generally agreed that increased awareness of the performance of all groups may be the most widely recognized accomplishment of standards-based reform, and particularly of the NCLB legislation.

Yet both the interview subjects and the workshop participants recognized the challenges of increasing equity in education and the limitations of what has been accomplished. The gaps have not been eliminated, and most agreed that reductions thus far have been fairly modest. Massell noted that according to a study by the Center on Education Policy (2007), gaps in most states remain substantial despite reductions, and some states have seen no reductions. Urban schools—those with the largest proportions of disadvantaged students—are the least likely to be meeting NCLB performance targets. Discussant Brian Stecher reinforced the concern that improvement has been modest, pointing out that "under the threat of severe sanctions from 'No Child Left Behind,' there is an unknown amount of inflation in test scores, and what we see in terms of gap closing on state tests is not always replicated in other low-stakes assessments." Many participants viewed the challenge of providing a truly equitable education for disadvantaged students as a central purpose of standards-based reform.

CAPACITY

The interview subjects viewed states' capacity to carry out all the improvements envisioned in standards-based reform as the most significant challenge to improving equity and achieving the other goals of standards-based reform, and workshop participants were quick to agree. The reforms have stretched state agencies and districts significantly during a period in which most have been losing personnel and resources. Massell noted that Massachusetts had 325 full-time staff by when its reforms were enacted into law in 1993, though it had had 990 employees just 13 years earlier. Smaller staffs have been responsible for developing new standards and aligning curriculum, instruction, and assessments to them. Other technical challenges, such as measuring the progress of English language learners in a valid manner, have increased the challenge of implementing the intended reforms.

NCLB required support of Title I schools (those serving specified percentages of low-income children) in specific ways. As growing numbers of schools and districts fall short of the NCLB performance targets, the strains on personnel are increasing. Fully 25 percent of schools across the country fell short of adequate yearly progress (AYP) targets in 2004-2005, and the numbers have been increasing since then, although Massell noted that that figure masks significant variation across states. For example, Florida and Alabama report that as many as 67 percent of their schools and 90 percent of their districts would fall short in 2008. Moreover, many states project that a cascading number of schools will be identified as underperforming in the coming years, as the law's 2014 deadline for having 100 percent of students perform at the proficient levels draws closer.

Capacity is critical to making a standards-based system perform as it is intended to. One necessary component of the strategy is data analysis, since, ideally, thoughtful analysis of timely data will guide teachers as they plan instruction; administrators as they plan teaching assignments, professional development, and many other aspects of their schools; and district and state staff as they make decisions about key questions such as curriculum planning and resource allocation. Yet as discussant Brian Stecher and others pointed out, teachers, administrators, and policy makers frequently lack either the training or the time—or both—to use the data they receive wisely. Few teachers have been adequately trained to use data to make improvements in instruction, and the annual testing data that is the most typical product of accountability systems are not particularly useful for that purpose.

More broadly, a number of participants stressed that standards-based accountability models provide a structure for identifying problems, but they do not directly address the challenges of bringing about better instruction. There is a risk that the standards-based reform model, and all of the testing and other time and resource intensive activities that are associated with it, may distract educators from one of the central challenges of reform: figuring out how to address the needs of disadvantaged students. As discussant Lynn Olson put it, one benefit of common standards could be to "force us to confront gross inequities," but educators and the public have known for decades that disadvantaged students are not doing well.

QUALITY

Building on the capacity issues, participants also discussed the gaps between the ideal model and reality. Discussant Lynn Olson noted that in the evaluation of state standards recently published by *Education Week*, not one state earned a top score on each of the criteria used, and many scored very poorly in a number of areas (Editorial Projects in Education, 2008). Stecher expanded on this point, arguing that very high standards are needed for the standards themselves. Because everything (including curriculum, textbooks, development of assessments, language for reporting results to the public) flows from the standards, they need not only to be clearly written and concise, but also to reflect current understanding of how children learn and their conceptual development. They also need to provide guidance about the performance criteria for determining whether students have mastered particular standards and guidance about the relative importance of the different elements included.

In practice, as the *Quality Counts* (Editorial Projects in Education, 2008) and other evaluations attest, state standards are not yet meeting those kinds of criteria. In the absence of the guidance that standards should provide, the default source for guidance is the assessment system. As Stecher put it: "We may be drifting toward assessment-based reform, rather than standards-based reform."

Yet the standards themselves may be the best developed aspect of the evolving reform systems. Participants called attention to persistent concerns about the nature, rigor, and quality of the assessments used in many states and about the narrowing effects they can have on curriculum and instruction. For example, few states systematically provide for extensive formative assessments that teachers could use to tailor instruction to individual students' needs. These kinds of concerns, many noted, suggest the potential benefits to states of greater uniformity among them. States could much more easily take advantage of one another's knowledge and experience and avoid duplication of effort if they were applying consistent frameworks.

This point was reinforced by questions about whether the multiple-standards model has yielded the consistency that was hoped for even within states. Researchers and policy makers from several states suggested that there is far more variation in both content and performance standards in practice than may be evident in states' written plans. As discussant Rae Ann Kelsch explained: "People are very reluctant to give up control." Although she spoke on the basis of the experience in North Dakota, which has not embraced standards wholeheartedly, others echoed her view. Standards-based systems have provided a model and a unifying conception of the purpose of education, "but very different goals can exist under the same banner" as one participant put it. Discussant Scott Montgomery said that the problem lies in changing the entire system, not just in unifying the standards, so for him common standards would not necessarily bring the changes that he believes are needed.

CURRENT STANDARDS: OVERVIEW

Committee chair Lorraine McDonnell reflected that the discussion of standards as they are currently operating yielded two significant paradoxes. The first paradox is that although standards are very well institutionalized across the country, with very few voices challenging their value as an organizing framework for reform, it is also the case that "standards-based reform" means different things to different people. The term in some ways disguises deep-seated differences about both priorities and strategies for achieving education goals.

The second paradox is that although there is little ostensible disagreement about the standards-based approach, there is a wide gap between the theoretical model and the reality of standards-based accountability systems in practice. The theoretical model of an aligned system is compelling as a strategy for meeting the needs of diverse students. Yet in practice, states and districts have lacked the capacity, resources, and perhaps in some cases, the knowledge or the will to put all the essential elements in place. Participants described legislators and other policy makers who have viewed the development of a new core curriculum or the raising of high school graduation standards as all that is required to pursue standards-based reform. Disputes over the significance of testing results, and the effects the reporting of these results can have, have further clouded the discussion.

2

Estimating Costs

With the complexity of implementing a standards-based accountability system in mind, the participants turned to the question of how one might estimate the costs of such a system to states. The committee had identified five framing questions to guide this discussion:

1. What are the major activities states undertake to develop and maintain a standards-based K-12 education system? What is the nature of the costs to states associated with each of these major activities?
2. What are the sources of variation in these costs by state?
3. What are the costs associated with each major activity across select states?
4. How much do state cost estimates vary for each activity?
5. What are the conceptual and technical issues involved in developing empirical estimates of these costs?

Margaret Goertz began the session with a proposed framework for considering the costs, providing an analysis of what states actually do in implementing a standards-based K-12 education system (Goertz, 2008). Douglas Harris and Lori Taylor followed with a detailed investigation of the challenges of estimating the costs of this kind of enterprise, as well as empirical estimates of the costs incurred in three states, Florida, North Dakota, and Texas (Harris and Taylor, 2008b).

BOX 2-1
Major Standards-Based Reform Activities

1. **Standards-setting**
   - Developing and revising academic content standards
   - Setting performance standards
   - Disseminating standards and training
2. **State Assessment**
   - Aligning assessment with standards
   - Item development
   - Test construction
   - Test administration
   - Test scoring
   - Score reporting
   - Technical review, validation of the system
3. **State Accountability System**
   - Data system (student, school, district)
   - Reporting (school, district)
   - Identifying school status, monitoring progress
   - Other accountability measures (process, etc.)
4. **Rewards and Sanctions**
   - Rewards to successful/improving schools
   - Sanctions for underperforming/failing districts, schools, or students
   - Intervention for failing schools, districts
   - Intervention for failing students

SOURCE: Goertz (2008).

COST ESTIMATION FRAMEWORK

Goertz organized her framework around what she identified as the six primary activities that comprise a standards-based reform system, though she noted that others might define the major activities differently; see Box 2-1. Goertz cautioned that the first four activities, which describe the mechanics of the standards themselves and the accountability system, generally receive most of the attention, but that the last two activities, which describe the ways in which the standards and accountability system may affect teaching and learning, are equally important.

Goertz used these six activities as the basis for a discussion of ways in which variation in implementation may affect the costs to states. Looking at the first three activities, she identified several primary sources of variation with cost implications. The frequency with which a state reviews and revises its standards and updates its assessments (as well as the number of subjects for which there are standards and the number of assessments) is one factor. A second factor is the process used for setting and reviewing content and performance standards, which varies in complexity, in part because of the number of people and groups involved. States may rely primarily on their department of education staff and volunteers, for example, or hire a contractor, use paid experts, or perhaps do all three.

With regard to rewards and sanctions (activity 4), there is a large range of approaches and of potential costs. Responses to classifications of schools or districts as falling short of the No Child Left Behind (NCLB) performance targets might begin with instructional audits or needs assessments. Interventions might include developing school improvement plans, measures to build capacity at the district level, or professional development in such areas as curriculum and instruction, data analysis, assessment, and leadership. For failing students, states vary in terms of how they determine eligibility and in how they structure and deliver remediation, as well as in how much funding may be available from the state for this purpose.

The characteristics of a state also play a significant role. Readily apparent differences, such as the size of a state and the demographics of its student population affect costs in predictable ways, but other factors are important as well. States vary in their mechanisms for funding public education and in the relative share that is paid by districts. States that have had standards-based reform policies for a decade or more are likely to have more firmly established systems and streamlined processes, which reduce costs. States with newer policies may thus have somewhat higher costs. A state's fiscal health also plays a role, perhaps because education budgets may remain more stable in the absence of economic downturns.

A key component of the variation in costs is the number of person hours required to accomplish the tasks involved. Salaries for regular staff, fees for consultants or contractors, and stipends for teachers who take on extra responsibilities are the prime costs for most of the activities. States also incur meeting and travel costs, as well as the costs of providing grants to districts, schools, or regional consortia. These are all costs that can be estimated, but Goertz noted that it is inherently more difficult to estimate the cost of a policy idea, such as standards-based reform, than a specific program.

Goertz returned to a point raised earlier, that standards-based reform is a term that can mean different things to different people. In order to estimate costs, one must determine which expenditures should be classed as standards-based reform costs and which are general K-12 education costs. One must also ask which costs would be incurred by states even without that conceptual approach and which are extra expenditures. Another complication is the task of distinguishing state costs from local costs. Since states' education funding formulas vary, the extent to which costs incurred at the local level are covered by state K-12 education funding can vary significantly—which makes it more difficult to compare across states.

APPLYING THE FRAMEWORK IN THREE STATES

Harris and Taylor began by echoing the points that standards-based reform is a complex idea and that developing cost estimates for an idea is inherently difficult. Thus, in their analysis of the costs they focused on two questions:

1. What costs are now being incurred by the nation to create, update, and minimally comply with standards, assessments, and accountability under current state and federal laws and rules?
2. What costs would the nation incur if the typical state system of standards, assessments, and accountability were replaced by a single common system?

To answer these questions, they first developed estimates of the costs of standards-based reform activities for three states—Florida, North Dakota, and Texas—that they viewed as reflecting a range in terms of size, education spending, and approaches to assessment and accountability.[1] Their notion was that since no one state could be viewed as representative or typical, they could use the data from these three states to compile a cost profile for a "typical state" and use that to calculate costs for the nation. They noted that their estimates are all based on the costs of simply complying with all requirements, rather than the costs of meeting goals, such as bringing all students to proficiency. They also cautioned that their work was preliminary and that they could not offer definitive estimates.[2]

The challenge of comparing the costs of the current system with those of a potential common system raises several economic concepts. One important distinction is that between fixed costs, those that are the same regardless of the scale of the program, and variable costs, those that vary depending on the scale. A significant fixed cost of standards-based reform is developing the content standards and setting the performance standards: this cost would be the same whether the standards

[1]The committee worked with Diane Massell and her colleagues and with Harris and Taylor to develop a list of states for analysis according to a variety of criteria, including geographic diversity, nature of standards and accountability program, and availability of cost data.

[2]Harris and Taylor subsequently completed their analysis and expanded on it for the second workshop.

were to apply to 100 students or 1 million. However, Harris explained, a common standard is likely to set a higher bar, which is likely to mean significant additional costs. Moreover, a substantial majority of the costs of standards-based reform are variable, and depend on design decisions (including how high the bar is set). Other variables would be the number of subjects and grade levels to be included, the frequency of assessment, the degree of support provided to schools, and the incentives and sanctions to be implemented.

Another distinction used by economists is that between opportunity costs and expenditures: reforms may switch resources from one activity to another and it is important to include such resource costs in the cost estimate, even if they do not result in new expenditures. So, for example, the time that teachers need to spend on testing-related tasks does not require additional state or district expenditures because the teachers would otherwise have been engaged in another task and would be receiving their salaries. However, there is a real resource cost in the loss of whatever they might otherwise have accomplished during that time. Harris and Taylor focused on these costs (they used the term "real resource costs" to avoid technical jargon) in order to capture that value.

Harris and Taylor highlighted some of the features of the three states' systems to illustrate more specifically the kinds of variation that affect costs. For example, Florida and Texas have both gone considerably beyond NCLB requirements (by testing at more grades and in more subjects), while North Dakota has not. Florida has a bonus program so that districts can give substantial monetary rewards to teachers for improvements made by their students, while Texas has a program to identify and accelerate certain students. Assigning the costs of these kinds of policies is complex, Harris explained, because one could argue that they are part of the cost of meeting the requirement—to push students toward proficiency—or one could argue that they are not required elements of a standards-based reform system. Moreover, a state government might reallocate resources in a way that poses a conundrum for cost estimators, for example, by switching instruction time from music to math. If making this change is not treated as a cost, the implication is that music instruction has no value. Assigning a dollar value to what is lost is not straightforward, but treating it as an additional cost may unreasonably inflate the overall estimate.

Having described some of the issues and assumptions that guided their work, Harris and Taylor presented their cost data. Their principal sources were national databases and data made publicly available by the three states. Their focus was to provide a rough comparative picture of the costs per pupil and per standard (e.g., 3rd-grade mathematics) of developing standards. The authors included both per-pupil and per-standards

TABLE 2-1 Preliminary Cost Estimates for Developing Standards in Three States

	Florida	North Dakota	Texas
Standards			
State	$37,853/standard	$15,385/standard	$21,853/standard
Local	$15.31/student	N/A	N/A
Assessments			
State-contracts	$15.10/student	$33.47/student	$20.46/student
State-admin	$10.21/student	$1.02/student	$2.38/student
Local	$20.72/student	$13.26/student	$12.60/student
Accountability			
State	N/A	$1.31/student	$1.60/student
Local	$0	$0	$0

NOTE: Estimates are the lower-bound estimates for real resource costs.
SOURCE: Harris and Taylor (2008a).

costs in order to capture both one-time (initial development) and annual costs (such as those for administering assessments). Their paper provides further detail about the costs they considered. Their preliminary cost estimates for the three states, which are tentative, they emphasized, are shown in Table 2-1. For context, annual expenditures for pre-K-12 education are $15.5 billion for Florida, which has 2,539,929 students; $711.0 million for North Dakota, which has 104,225 students; and $28.2 billion for Texas, which has 4,259,823 students (http://www.edweek.org/rc/states/ [April 2008]).

None of these three states could be viewed as typical, but North Dakota came closest to approximating the situation for a state that is meeting, but not going beyond, the legal requirements and rules. Harris and Taylor have developed a plan for breaking the North Dakota costs into the fixed and variable categories in order to adjust those estimates for use as the typical state. They had not completed this complex analysis in time for the workshop. Nevertheless, their preliminary response to question 1, regarding the costs of current systems, is that the costs of standards-based assessment and accountability systems is a relatively small percentage of total educational costs.

Harris and Taylor's portrait of the complexity of estimating costs and identifying potential savings that could be achieved with a model based on common standards stimulated a range of reactions. Discussant Thomas Toch was struck by how small the investment has been. He argued that standardized tests have become, by default, the central driver of standards-based reform, the mechanism that largely determines what is taught and when and how it is taught. Yet of the average $8,000 spent per pupil annually, only one-half of 1 percent goes toward building the tests that are to measure progress toward the high standards that are widely supported. From his perspective, a move to common standards and tests would, by reducing the significant financial burden to states of developing their own standards and assessment programs, free resources for other targeted investments in improving teaching and learning.

Discussant Susan Traiman also voiced concerns about the quality of the existing system. She questioned the usefulness of estimating the cost of producing systems that have received relatively low marks for quality, referring not just to the three states that were analyzed, but to all 50. She was also concerned that the approach Harris and Taylor used did not account for relative quality among states' standards, pointing out that a state with a smaller number of very focused, thoughtfully developed, standards might have a higher per-standard cost than a state with a multitude of standards. She argued that a more critical question was what kinds of resources the nation and the states are willing to invest to make sure that all students meet rigorous standards.

Other participants added to this point, noting that what would be of most interest would be a sense of the cost of developing common standards that had the effect of helping more students meet high standards. To calculate the cost in that way would mean including the costs for such interventions as professional development courses and new instructional materials.

In their paper, Harris and Taylor (2008b) had addressed two additional categories of costs that could be analyzed. The first is what they termed necessary but nonrequired costs, such as periodic assessments used by districts to monitor students' progress toward the benchmarks as measured by standardized tests. They developed tentative estimates that districts spend an average of $5 to $10 per student on these supplementary assessments. The second category was what they called "apparently new resources," the costs of making changes in teacher preparation and certification, curriculum, textbook selection, and other system elements in order to align them with standards. While these two additional categories may not capture the full scope of the investment needed to implement standards-based reform that addresses persistent achievement gaps and raises achievement to desired levels, they do point toward additional analyses that could be helpful.

Discussant Dave Driscoll pointed out additional costs that could be considered in light of the earlier discussion about resources and capacity. One example is the cost to Massachusetts of releasing every single test item that is used so that the process is completely transparent to students, parents, and the public: doing so increases the cost substantially (other states bank many items for reuse), but it has important political and practical benefits. Driscoll also noted that "at the beginning we had plenty of money . . . the legislature provided whatever we needed." Over time, however, budgets have been squeezed. The Massachusetts legislature had initially provided extra funds to support students who were in danger of failing the high school graduation test, but as first-time pass rates passed 80 percent, those funds were discontinued.

Discussant Mark Harris considered the capacity issue from a qualitative perspective. He observed that although states prize their autonomy and flexibility in developing systems that will best serve their students, many nevertheless base much of their instruction on commercially available programs that have very little link to state standards. These programs are often designed to provide so-called "teacher-proof" curricula and instructional plans and thus do very little to develop the capacities of teachers who use them or to push the state-specific education goals forward.

Participants proposed many potential costs that had not been considered in the analysis, while acknowledging both the complexity of developing the estimates and their value as a starting point for discussion. Laurie Wise summed up the message that many drew from the consideration of costs with a reminder of the fundamental question: "Is what we are investing in actually helping students to meet these standards, not just in defining and measuring them?"

3

Analyzing State Standards

Similarities and differences among states' content and performance standards are key to understanding the extent to which any move toward more common standards would have a substantive impact on current standards-based systems. An examination of states' approaches was organized around three framing questions:

1. How and to what extent do K-12 state content standards in English/language arts, mathematics, and science at key grades vary?
2. How and to what extent to K-12 state performance standards in English/language arts, mathematics, and science at key grades vary?
3. How and to what extent does the implementation of K-12 state content and performance standards in multiple academic subjects in classrooms vary?

Analysis of both content and performance standards provided the foundation for an extensive discussion of these questions. Andrew Porter and his colleagues described a very detailed review of 31 states' standards in the three subjects, with a focus on grades 4 and 8, which was developed for the workshop. Michael Petrilli described an analysis conducted by the Fordham Foundation and the Northwest Evaluation Association (NWEA) to compare proficiency standards across states. Peggy Carr closed the session with a description of the results of an analysis by the National Center for Education Statistics (NCES) of the relationship between proficiency standards for state assessments and those the National Assessment of Educational Progress (NAEP).[1]

VARIABILITY IN STATE CONTENT STANDARDS

Porter and his colleagues addressed the first question by analyzing state content standards in English/language arts/reading, mathematics, and science for grades K-8 (Porter, Polikoff, and Smithson, 2008). Their analysis was based on a conceptual framework for considering the primary influences on teachers' instructional practices. Their hypothesis is that teachers are most strongly influenced by standards policies that have five characteristics:

1. They are specific in their messages to teachers about what they are to teach.
2. They are consistent (aligned) among themselves so that teachers receive a coherent message.
3. They have authority, in that they are developed and promoted by experts, are officially adopted by the state, are consistent with standards practice, and are promoted by charismatic individuals (meaning individuals who provide leadership and motivate those who must implement the standards).
4. They have power, in that compliance with them is rewarded while failure to comply is sanctioned.
5. They have stability, in that they are kept in place over time.

The team also based their analysis on a methodology that Porter and his colleagues had developed for describing in detail what it is that teachers teach, which they have called a three-dimensional content language. Although this methodology actually predated the standards-based reform movement, it has proved a useful tool for examining the content of state standards documents.

Porter described the method as a way of producing a visual representation of the relative coverage of various elements of a particular field that is similar to a topographical map of a geographical region. Using the content language, Porter and his colleagues have divided each subject into general areas. For example, in mathematics there are 16 general areas (e.g., operations, measurement, basic algebra), and each of these can be further

[1]The term "proficiency standards" refers to the level of performance identified on a particular test as the minimum that qualifies as "proficient." Thus, it is a type of performance standard.

subdivided into between 9 and 14 more specific topics—for a total of 217. Apart from the subtopics that make up each field, the language also distinguishes levels of cognitive demand, which are also somewhat different for each subject. There are eight cognitive levels for mathematics: memorize; perform procedures; demonstrate understanding, conjecture; generalize; prove; solve novel problems; and make connections. Thus, Porter explained, content is defined as the intersection of these two dimensions. Using this tool, for example, one can determine not just whether or not linear equations are covered, but also whether students will be expected to memorize one, solve one, or use one to solve a story problem.

To apply this language analysis to a state's standards, trained analysts review and code the most specific available description of the standard for a particular subject and grade level. Each standard is analyzed by three to five analysts, and items that are difficult to code are flagged and discussed. The codes are entered into cells as proportions, with 0 representing no emphasis and 1 representing a very strong focus. The cells are used to build the visual display that illustrates both the degree of focus on the various topics and the cognitive demand.

Porter and his colleagues drew on data from 31 states, though not all provided data for every subject and grade level. The team also analyzed the national science standards and those of the National Council of Teachers of Mathematics (NCTM). They focused on grades 4 and 8, with the goal of highlighting the degree to which states' standards showed overlap or conceptual progressions between those two grades. Having entered the codes, they were able to conduct a variety of analyses and comparisons.

For any pair of states for which they had data, the alignment for a particular standard can be calculated. Using averages of these results, they were also able to calculate alignment across and within grade levels.

From the example in Figure 3-1, which shows the results for the two states that are most aligned in English/language arts/reading for 4th grade, it is clear that content areas such as vocabulary, comprehension, and language study (the darkest areas) are strongly emphasized in both Ohio and Indiana and that neither state places any emphasis on phonemic awareness. Moreover, both states clearly focused on the capacity to explain as their target level of cognitive demand. Figure 3-2 shows the mapping for one of the areas of strong alignment, comprehension, by its subcategories.

The team also looked at degrees of variance, as shown in Table 3-1, which depicts the degree of alignment among 14 states in English/language arts/reading for grades 4 and 8. The results show significant variation, from lows such as the 0.07 correlation between Maine and Wisconsin for grade 8, to highs such as 0.47 between Ohio and California for grade 8. Tables 3-2 and 3-3 show the degree of alignment among the states'

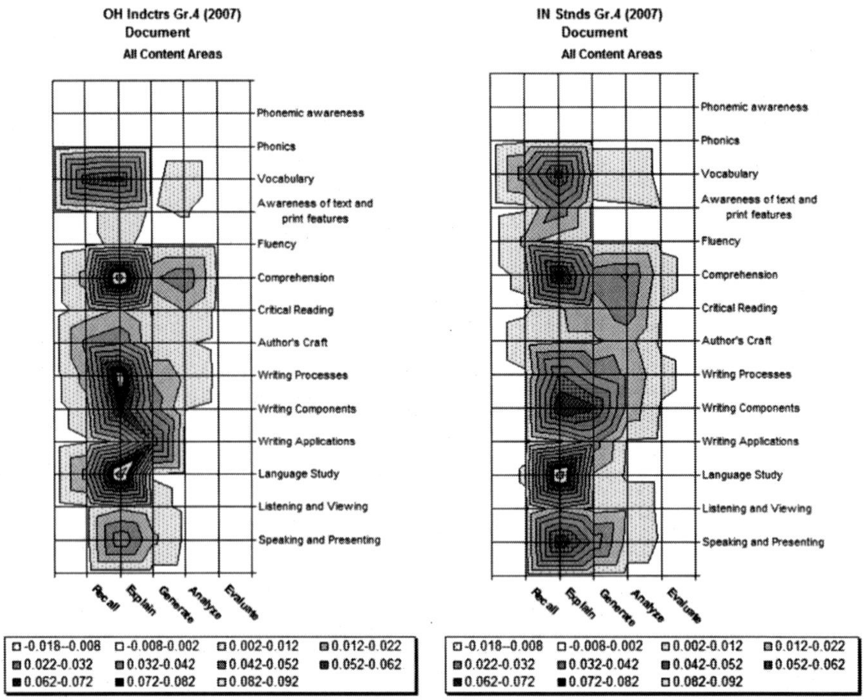

Alignment = .48

FIGURE 3-1 Coarse-grained content maps: English/language arts/reading for grade 4.
SOURCE: Porter, Polikoff, and Smithson (2008, Figure 1).

standards and the national science standards (5 states), and the NCTM standards (10 states). In all, Porter and his colleagues have produced a voluminous body of data: 90 figures, 10 tables, and an appendix.[2]

Porter explained that although it would be much easier if these data could be simplified, he and his colleagues could find no substitute for the fine-grained analysis for answering the questions at hand. Nevertheless, some key general points were evident. First, they found little evidence to support the hypothesis that there is a *de facto* national curriculum. The degree of variability they found across states, and between state and national standards, does not support that hypothesis. In fact, they found

[2]The material is available at http://www7.nationalacademies.org/cfe/State_Standards_Workshop_1_Agenda.html [May 2008].

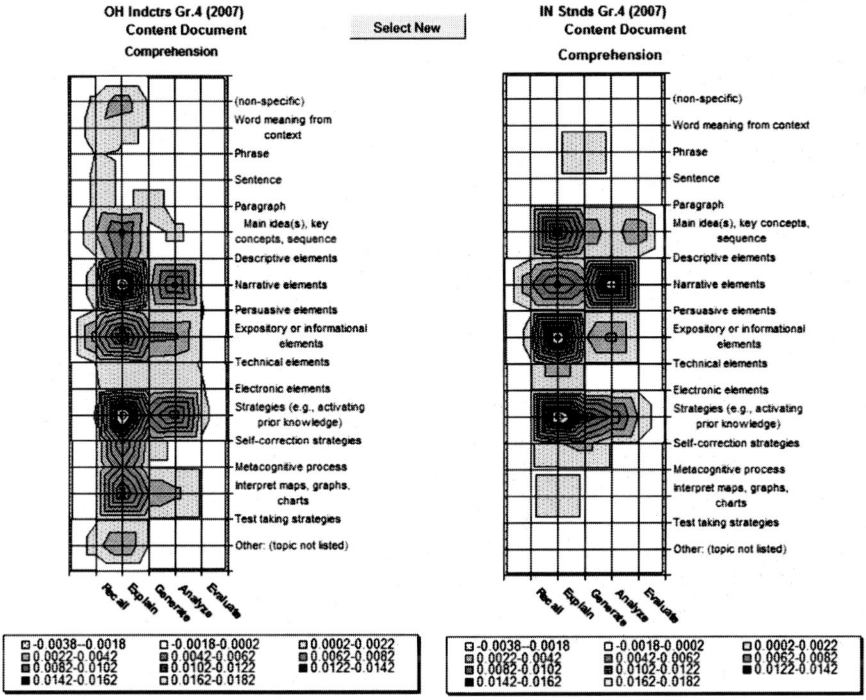

FIGURE 3-2 Fine-grained content maps for comprehension: English/language arts/reading for grade 4.
SOURCE: Porter, Polikoff, and Smithson (2008, Figure 22).

that the alignment of topic coverage within states from grade to grade (the degree of overlap in what is in the standards for each grade, as students ostensibly progress) is generally greater than the degree of alignment across states in the material they cover at particular grades. The repetition, Porter suggested, sends students the message: "Don't you dare learn this the first time we teach it; otherwise you are going to be bored out of your skull in the subsequent grades."

Porter and his colleagues did find some indication that there are a few core areas that are covered more consistently across states than the overall alignment data would show—or a small *de facto* common core curriculum. However, Porter and his colleagues also concluded that states' content standards are in general not focused on a few big ideas. Though the states

TABLE 3-1 State-to-State Alignment, 4th and 8th Grade Standards for English/Language Arts/Reading (ELAR)

	CA Stnds Gr.4	DE GLEs Gr.4	ID Stnds Gr.4	IN Stnds Gr.4	KS Stnds Gr.4	ME GLEs Gr.4	MN ELAR Stnds. Gr.4	MT R Stnds Gr.4	NH Reading GLEs Gr.4	OH Indctrs Gr.4	OK Stnds Gr.4	OR Stnds Gr.4	VT GLEs Gr.4	WI Stnds Gr.4
CA Stnds Gr.4 (2005)	1.00	0.14	0.26	0.40	0.12	0.11	0.38	0.23	0.09	0.30	0.43	0.33	0.31	0.32
DE GLEs Gr.4 (2006)	0.14	1.00	0.09	0.16	0.13	0.11	0.17	0.19	0.11	0.16	0.17	0.19	0.15	0.16
ID Stnds Gr.4 (2006)	0.26	0.09	1.00	0.28	0.13	0.11	0.30	0.14	0.15	0.22	0.31	0.29	0.27	0.26
IN Stnds Gr.4 (2007)	0.40	0.16	0.28	1.00	0.14	0.18	0.38	0.17	0.19	0.48	0.34	0.42	0.35	0.30
KS Stnds Gr.4 (2005)	0.12	0.13	0.13	0.14	1.00	0.21	0.19	0.30	0.24	0.14	0.20	0.22	0.18	0.13
ME GLEs Gr.4 (2005)	0.11	0.11	0.11	0.18	0.21	1.00	0.14	0.19	0.23	0.18	0.16	0.18	0.17	0.11
MN ELAR Stnds. Gr.4 (2005)	0.38	0.17	0.30	0.38	0.19	0.14	1.00	0.28	0.18	0.33	0.45	0.42	0.42	0.30
MT R Stnds Gr.4 (2005)	0.23	0.19	0.14	0.17	0.30	0.19	0.28	1.00	0.19	0.19	0.25	0.25	0.22	0.22
NH Reading GLEs Gr.4 (2005)	0.09	0.11	0.15	0.19	0.24	0.23	0.18	0.19	1.00	0.13	0.12	0.18	0.17	0.13
OH Indctrs Gr.4 (2007)	0.30	0.16	0.22	0.48	0.14	0.18	0.33	0.19	0.13	1.00	0.29	0.39	0.31	0.30
OK Stnds Gr.4 (2005)	0.43	0.17	0.31	0.34	0.20	0.16	0.45	0.25	0.12	0.29	1.00	0.37	0.34	0.32
OR Stnds Gr.4 (2007)	0.33	0.19	0.29	0.42	0.22	0.18	0.42	0.25	0.18	0.39	0.37	1.00	0.39	0.28
VT GLEs Gr.4 (2006)	0.31	0.15	0.27	0.35	0.18	0.17	0.42	0.22	0.17	0.31	0.34	0.39	1.00	0.27
WI Stnds Gr.4 (2003)	0.32	0.16	0.26	0.30	0.13	0.11	0.30	0.22	0.13	0.30	0.32	0.28	0.27	1.00
	CA Stnds Gr.8	**DE GLEs Gr.8**	**ID Stnds Gr.8**	**IN Stnds Gr.8**	**KS Stnds Gr.8**	**ME GLEs Gr.8**	**MN ELAR Stnds. Gr.8**	**MT R Stnds Gr.8**	**NH Reading GLEs Gr.8**	**OH Indctrs Gr.8**	**OK Stnds Gr.8**	**OR Stnds Gr.8**	**VT GLEs Gr.8**	**WI Stnds Gr.8**
CA Stnds Gr.8 (2005)	1.00	0.28	0.31	0.35	0.39	0.12	0.46	0.22	0.21	0.47	0.13	0.43	0.39	0.38
DE GLEs Gr.8 (2005)	0.28	1.00	0.26	0.25	0.24	0.24	0.30	0.32	0.26	0.23	0.15	0.29	0.27	0.18
ID Stnds Gr.8 (2006)	0.31	0.26	1.00	0.29	0.31	0.13	0.34	0.13	0.18	0.32	0.11	0.40	0.31	0.26
IN Stnds Gr.8 (2006)	0.35	0.25	0.29	1.00	0.29	0.09	0.34	0.15	0.17	0.28	0.12	0.34	0.28	0.24
KS Stnds Gr.8 (2003)	0.39	0.24	0.31	0.29	1.00	0.16	0.37	0.24	0.24	0.38	0.15	0.38	0.39	0.24
ME GLEs Gr.8 (2005)	0.12	0.24	0.13	0.09	0.16	1.00	0.12	0.24	0.24	0.10	0.15	0.18	0.13	0.07
MN ELAR Stnds. Gr.8 (2005)	0.46	0.30	0.34	0.34	0.37	0.12	1.00	0.23	0.29	0.47	0.23	0.48	0.41	0.32
MT R Stnds Gr.8 (2005)	0.22	0.32	0.13	0.15	0.24	0.24	0.23	1.00	0.23	0.18	0.19	0.20	0.19	0.15
NH Reading GLEs Gr.8 (2005)	0.21	0.26	0.18	0.17	0.24	0.24	0.29	0.23	1.00	0.20	0.22	0.24	0.22	0.10
OH Indctrs Gr.8 (2005)	0.47	0.23	0.32	0.28	0.38	0.10	0.47	0.18	0.20	1.00	0.12	0.40	0.38	0.33
OK Stnds Gr.8 (2007)	0.13	0.15	0.11	0.12	0.15	0.15	0.23	0.19	0.22	0.12	1.00	0.19	0.18	0.08
OR Stnds Gr.8 (2007)	0.43	0.29	0.40	0.34	0.38	0.18	0.48	0.20	0.24	0.40	0.19	1.00	0.43	0.30
VT GLEs Gr.8 (2006)	0.39	0.27	0.31	0.28	0.39	0.13	0.41	0.19	0.22	0.38	0.18	0.43	1.00	0.22
WI Stnds Gr.8 (2003)	0.38	0.18	0.26	0.24	0.24	0.07	0.32	0.15	0.10	0.33	0.08	0.30	0.22	1.00

SOURCE: Porter, Polikoff, and Smithson (2008, Table 1).

TABLE 3-2 Alignment Among States for the National Science Standards for Grades 1-8

	CA Stnds Gr. 1-8	DE Stnds Gr. 1-8	IN Stnds Gr. 1-8	OK Stnds Gr. 1-8	NSE Stnds Gr. K-8
CA Stnds Gr. 1-8	1.00	0.25	0.20	0.27	0.22
DE Stnds Gr. 1-8	0.25	1.00	0.40	0.44	0.39
IN Stnds Gr. 1-8	0.20	0.40	1.00	0.41	0.50
OK Stnds Gr. 1-8	0.27	0.44	0.41	1.00	0.38
NSE Stnds Gr. K-8	0.22	0.39	0.50	0.38	1.00

SOURCE: Porter, Polikoff, and Smithson (2008, Table 6).

vary in this as well, overall their standards do not demonstrate the clear focus and discipline that many have advocated.

VARIABILITY IN STATE ASSESSMENTS

Assessing the extent to which the performance standards that states set come close to defining a *de facto* common standard for proficiency was the impetus behind another study, described by Michael Petrilli. This study, conducted jointly by the Fordham Foundation and NWEA, was designed to address three questions:

1. Where are states setting the proficiency bar, and can states' approaches to setting cut scores be compared in a fair way?
2. Given the pressure to bring 100 percent of students to proficient levels, are states lowering their standards over time in order to meet that goal?
3. Are cut scores relatively consistent in terms of difficulty level across grades?

Fordham and the NWEA decided to collaborate to conduct this study because the NWEA develops a computer-adaptive assessment system that is used by many districts. The test is used primarily for diagnostic testing so that districts can pinpoint the performance levels of individual students in different areas that are covered in the relevant state standards. Thus, the assessment is designed to be as well aligned as possible to the content standards of the states in which it is used. NWEA maintains a large pool of items, and they construct tests for districts by using the items that are closest to the standards for which that district is responsible. Because all the items are pegged to a common scale, NWEA is able to make some comparisons across states.

TABLE 3-3 Alignment Among States on Mathematics Standards for Grades 1-8

	DE GLEs Gr.1-8	ID Stnds Gr. 1-8	IN Stnds Gr. 1-8	KS Stnds Gr. 1-8	MN Stnds Gr. 1-8	NH Stnds Gr. 1-8	OH Stnds Gr. 1-8	OK Stnds Gr. 1-8	OR Stnds Gr. 1-8	VT Stnds Gr. 1-8	NCTM Stnds Gr. K-8
DE GLEs Gr.1-8	1.00	0.49	0.50	0.54	0.50	0.41	0.56	0.48	0.55	0.53	0.54
ID Stnds Gr. 1-8	0.49	1.00	0.46	0.49	0.40	0.40	0.46	0.42	0.48	0.43	0.39
IN Stnds Gr. 1-8	0.50	0.46	1.00	0.51	0.40	0.40	0.52	0.47	0.56	0.46	0.43
KS Stnds Gr. 1-8	0.54	0.49	0.51	1.00	0.39	0.48	0.57	0.45	0.58	0.49	0.41
MN Stnds Gr. 1-8	0.50	0.40	0.40	0.39	1.00	0.39	0.44	0.37	0.43	0.39	0.38
NH Stnds Gr. 1-8	0.41	0.40	0.40	0.48	0.39	1.00	0.46	0.36	0.45	0.53	0.35
OH Stnds Gr. 1-8	0.56	0.46	0.52	0.57	0.44	0.46	1.00	0.46	0.62	0.53	0.41
OK Stnds Gr. 1-8	0.48	0.42	0.47	0.45	0.37	0.36	0.46	1.00	0.48	0.40	0.45
OR Stnds Gr. 1-8	0.55	0.48	0.56	0.58	0.43	0.45	0.62	0.48	1.00	0.51	0.38
VT Stnds Gr. 1-8	0.53	0.43	0.46	0.49	0.39	0.53	0.53	0.40	0.51	1.00	0.49
NCTM Stnds Gr. K-8	0.54	0.39	0.43	0.41	0.38	0.35	0.41	0.45	0.38	0.49	1.00

SOURCE: Porter, Polikoff, and Smithson (2008, Table 7).

With this resource, the researchers were able to estimate where on the NWEA scale a given state is setting its cut score. In many cases they had that calculation for two times, 2003 and 2006, and were thus able to consider the possibility that the cut scores had changed over time in those states. They had data for a total of 830,000 students in 26 states who had taken both NWEA's assessment and their own state exam.

The researchers' primary finding was that there is enormous variability in the level of difficulty of states' tests—a range from approximately the 6th percentile (94 percent would pass) to approximately the 77th percentile (23 percent would pass). These findings are shown in Figure 3-3.

To illustrate the kinds of differences these numbers represent, Petrilli provided two sample 4th-grade items from the NWEA assessment, each with a difficulty level at the cut score of one of the states. For the Wisconsin cut score, which they had calculated at the 16th percentile on the NWEA scale, the sample item asked students to select from a group of sentences the one that "tells a fact, not an opinion." To represent the comparable cut score for Massachusetts, calculated at the 65th percentile, Petrilli showed an item that asked students to read a complex, difficult passage (excerpted from a work by Leo Tolstoy) and to pick from a list of factual statements the one that is actually found in the passage.

Petrilli believes the implications of this degree of difference are profound. If, as many people believe, the high stakes attached to state tests mean that teachers focus the bulk of their attention on the students who are just below the proficient level, to get them over that bar, then teachers in Wisconsin will be targeting their instruction at a very low level in comparison with those in Massachusetts. This analytical approach also made it possible to compare the cut scores that states set for math and for reading, at least in terms of percentiles. Doing so is useful, Petrilli explained, because test results that seem to demonstrate that students are doing better in one subject that the other, may actually demonstrate that the level of mastery needed to score at the proficient level is quite different for each subject.

With regard to the second question, whether states are engaged in a so-called race to the bottom, the researchers were surprised to find that this does not seem to be the case. Rather, Petrilli characterized the trend as a "walk to the middle." Most states had kept their cut scores relatively consistent across the time period studied, but the states that began with the highest standards had moderated their standards somewhat, while those with the lowest standards had raised theirs. He cautioned, however, that because they were working with percentiles, the change over time could be explained either by intentional shifts in cut scores or by changes in students' actual achievement levels.

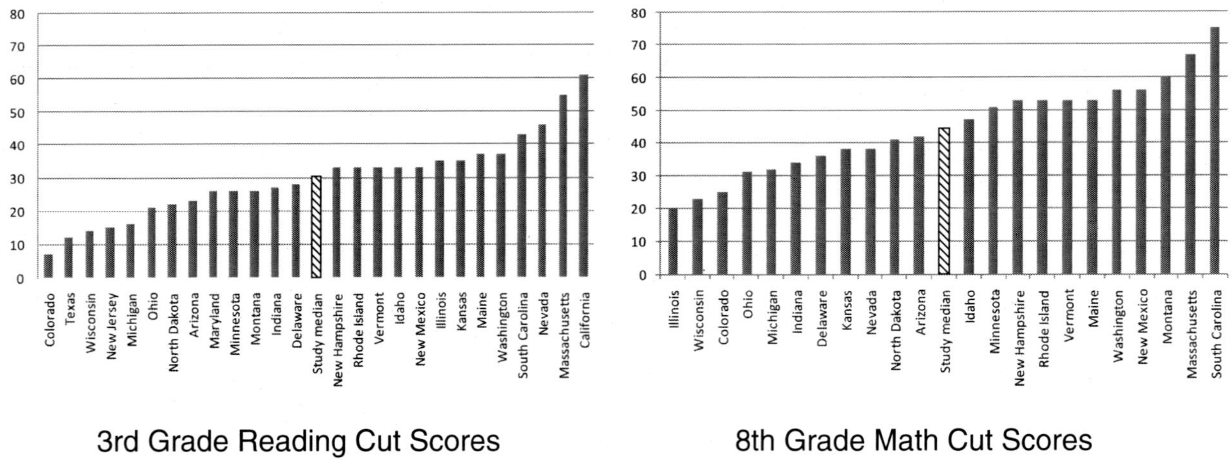

FIGURE 3-3 Difference in difficulty of state tests.
SOURCE: Petrilli (2008).

In terms of the last question, the vertical alignment of state standards, the analysis showed that they are not well calibrated, grade level to grade level. In the majority of states, the elementary standards are set significantly lower than the middle school standards. Where this is the case, students may have no trouble with the 3rd-grade test, proceed normally through subsequent grades, and then stumble on the 8th-grade test. The aggregate results may inaccurately indicate a problem with middle school instruction, in comparison with elementary school instruction. Moreover, if standards are not aligned vertically, the test results will not be good indicators of students' growth over time.

Petrilli drew three conclusions from the research. First, state performance standards need "an overhaul." If the goal is for standards to progress cumulatively from kindergarten through 12th grade, states should begin with rigorous high school graduation requirements and work backward to develop vertically aligned standards. Second, Petrilli believes that the objective of bringing 100 percent of students to proficiency has become a perverse incentive that has the effect of lowering achievement. Finally, in responding to the workshop theme, he said that discussion of common standards should continue—that such discussion would have the effect of creating consistent objectives for students across the states.

VARIABILITY IN STATE PERFORMANCE STANDARDS

NAEP is also used as a common yardstick for comparing students' proficiency across states. The No Child Left Behind Act requires not only that states report progress on their own assessments, but also that they participate in NAEP so that comparisons can be made. The results of such comparisons indicate striking discrepancies between the performance required for proficiency on state assessments and what is required for proficiency on NAEP assessments. These results have received significant public attention and, as presenter Peggy Carr explained, NCES recognized the need for a more precise methodology with which to make these comparisons (see National Center for Education Statistics, 2007).

Figure 3-4 illustrates the discrepancies between the proficiency levels states use to report their adequate yearly progress and the NAEP proficiency levels, in terms of percentages of students meeting the standard.

This information is useful to provide a snapshot, Carr explained. Since each state is asked to use NAEP as a benchmark, the comparison between each state and NAEP is valid. However, comparing states just by using the percentage meeting the standard is less useful. Consequently, NCES staff used an equipercentile equating method to align the distributions of pairs of scales, the NAEP scale and that of each of the states. In other words, they used results from schools that had participated in

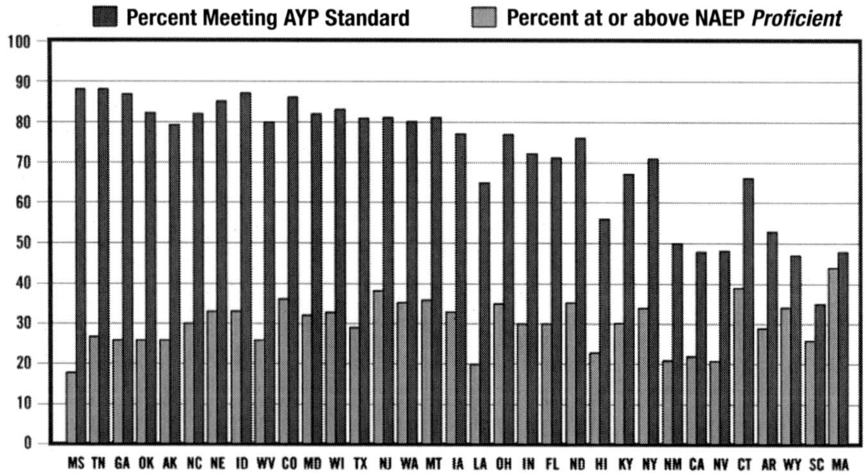

FIGURE 3-4 A comparison of state proficiency and NAEP standards.
SOURCE: Carr (2008).

NAEP to calculate what they called a NAEP-equivalent score on the state assessment. Having done that for each state, they could then compare the NAEP-equivalent scores of any state to that of any other. What the comparison shows is the relative degree of challenge of a state's standards using the NAEP scale as the common yardstick. Figure 3-5 shows how the comparison works for two sample states.

The results of this analysis were quite similar to the results of the Fordham NWEA analysis. Generally, the researchers found that states' proficiency levels varied significantly and that the majority map onto the "below basic" range on the NAEP scale, though the distribution varied by subject and grade. The results for mathematics are shown in Figures 3-6 and 3-7.

The researchers also looked at the correlation between the proportion of students that a state reports as meeting its proficiency standards and the NAEP-equivalent score. They found that the correlation was negative: that is, the higher the number of students that a state reports are passing its own standards, the less challenging are that state's standards. The researchers also found that the position of a state's adequate yearly progress standards on the NAEP scale bears little relationship to that state's performance on the NAEP assessment. In other words, students' performance on NAEP cannot be predicted from the relative difficulty of the state's own standards.

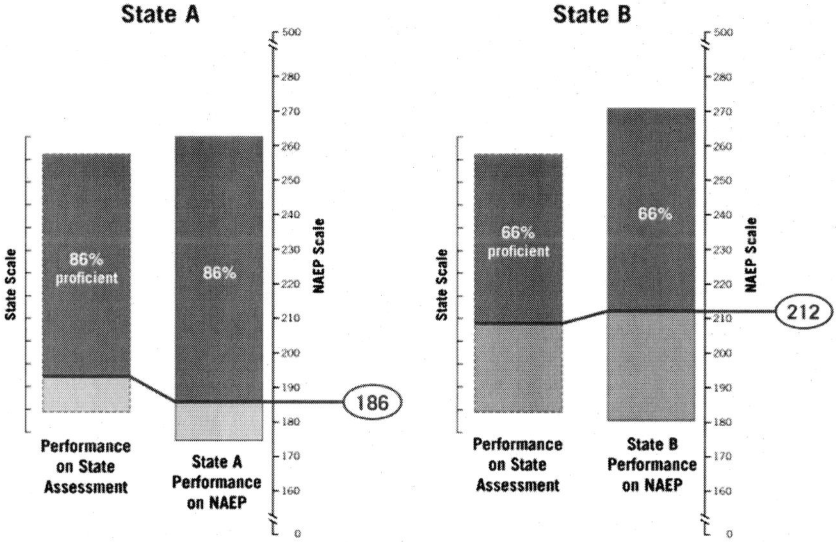

FIGURE 3-5 Methodology for comparing state proficiency standards.
SOURCE: Carr (2008).

Carr's conclusions from these results were similar to Petrilli's. To illustrate their significance, she highlighted the results for three contiguous states, Georgia, North Carolina, and South Carolina. Students in these three states all perform at about the same level on the NAEP reading assessment, but the states have set very different standards for their students. An example of the practical effect of this discrepancy is that a student who, moves from North Carolina to South Carolina might go from being viewed as a proficient reader to being placed in a remedial class.

Carr closed by noting that state assessments vary widely in both content and design, and that states may attach different meanings to the label "proficient." In the context of NAEP, proficiency is defined as "competency over challenging subject matter"; in contrast, states generally define proficiency as on grade-level performance.

Discussant Barbara Reys drew on her experiences cochairing the standards development process for mathematics in Missouri to highlight some of the practical challenges of working toward common standards. Apart from the requirements of states that prize their autonomy, she noted the limitations of existing national standards, which may not be grade specific and lack other critical details. She was not surprised at the finding that many states' standards do not align with national ones because "it's

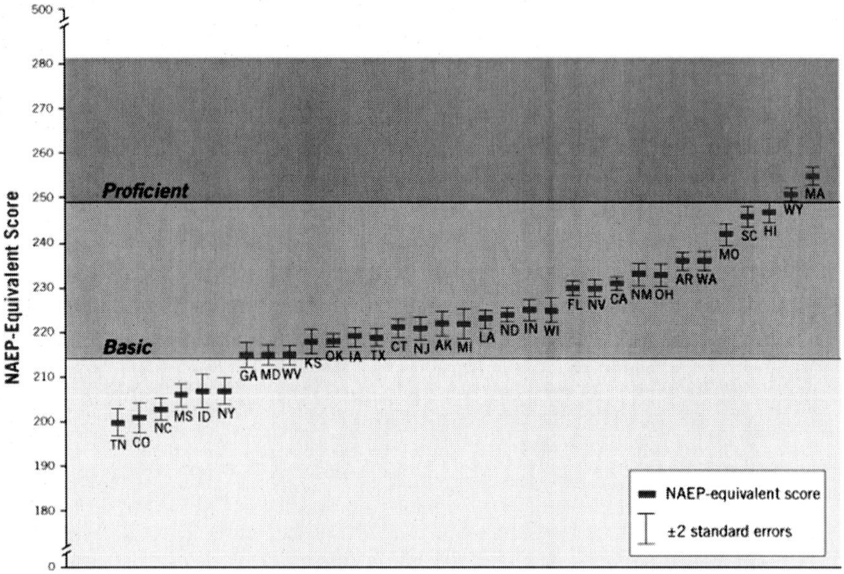

FIGURE 3-6 A comparison of proficiency standards in grade 4 mathematics.
SOURCE: Carr (2008).

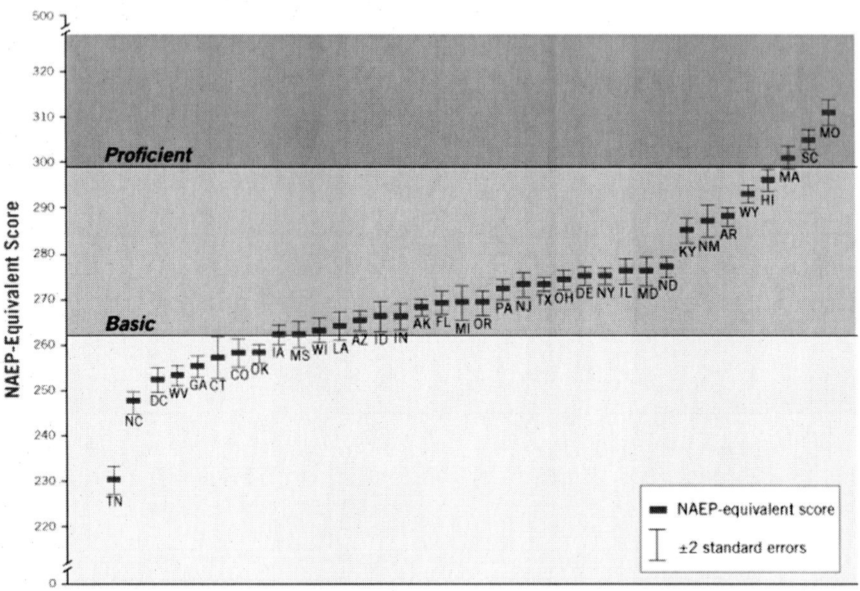

FIGURE 3-7 A comparison of proficiency standards in grade 8 mathematics.
SOURCE: Carr (2008).

really the decisions about what you want to focus on at particular grades that are the tough ones."

Reys also showed some results from an analysis of consistency she had conducted of K-8 mathematics standards. Her findings echoed those already presented. She found dramatic variation from state to state in the grade placement of particular concepts. The critical finding was again that a given learning expectation might be found in the first grade standards in one state and in the third grade standards in another state.

These differences create a significant complication for textbook publishers who want to serve multiples states. From Reys' analysis, only 4 of 108 possible learning expectations for 4th graders were common across ten states—suggesting that a textbook publisher might choose to incorporate all 108 of them. Since the content of textbooks has a significant effect on teachers' instructional plans, this lack of overlap becomes a self-reinforcing pressure against curricular focus. At the same time, however, textbooks are a potential tool for increasing uniformity because they are so influential.

Discussant William Schmidt characterized the variation among state standards as "enormous." He believes that both math and science standards display "the maximum possible variation at every combination of grade level and topic." He suggested that this is particularly bad for mathematics because that subject has an inherent logic, so that it is essential that students learn concepts in a particular order if they are to develop sound mathematical thinking. The problem, he said, is that because so few standards establish coherence and vertical alignment in mathematics goals, the result is a mishmash, with many concepts being introduced far too early and then repeated over and over in subsequent grades. Ironically, he explained, the topics that get the least coverage tend to be the most important—the deeper topics that build conceptual understanding.

Schmidt has also observed that district standards vary as much as those of states. Moreover, he suggested, variation at the classroom level, in terms of what teachers are actually covering with their students, far outpaces the variation at the district and state levels. For Schmidt, this variation, which permeates the entire education system, is "the Achilles heel of the No Child Left Behind Act." Based on his analysis, he argued that the degree of variation in the opportunities children have to learn makes it inevitable that many will be left behind.

Discussant Peter McWalters offered a perspective from Rhode Island, which has coordinated its standards development with three other states, Maine, New Hampshire, and Vermont. Although the presentations suggested a number of questions for this consortium of states to ponder as they work to improve their standards, he labeled the effort a success and added that he would be happy to see a national model. He noted that

NCLB had been the impetus for the efforts of the New England states because none of the four has a testing infrastructure and all are too small to produce what is required on their own. They were also fortunate in that none of them has regulatory roadblocks, such as state-mandated standards, so working collectively was relatively easy.

However, McWalters identified what he sees a major stumbling block to a national approach to standards, that "no state would trust the feds after our experience with the beginning of No Child Left Behind. . . . There is zero trust." He also supported points made earlier regarding states' capacity to change in the ways that are needed. For him, the biggest challenge is in finding ways to serve diverse students with diverse needs. To do that successfully, teachers will need a command of their subjects—the content and the pedagogy that is "way beyond what we currently have."

4

Wrap-Up and Next Steps

For the workshop's final session, participants were asked to reflect about the key messages from each of the workshop sessions and to identify topics and issues the committee should address in its second workshop. In preparation for this session, the participants had met in smaller, breakout groups. Each of the breakout groups came up with long lists of important take-away messages, as well as questions they identified for more discussion. There was significant overlap among the groups, who offered many ideas for the committee to consider.

VARIABILITY OF STANDARDS

- There is significant variability among states in the nature of their content standards, what is covered, and the performance levels they set. No clear consensus has emerged in the field as to the effects of the variation, though some view the variation itself as a major impediment to equity. Consistent standards may be a necessary tool for ensuring educational equity, but simply establishing them will not accomplish the goal. More information is needed about why states approach the issue so differently and the effects that these differences have on student learning.
- The variation in proficiency standards highlights the limitations of a model that focuses on achievement to a particular defined level. Many argue that a growth model (an assessment system that focuses on measuring students' academic growth over time)

may be a more useful approach than a model that provides snapshots of the percentages who have reached a particular level.

- There may be as much variation in the ways different districts in a state implement standards (perhaps even among classrooms within a school) as there is among states. It is not clear whether common standards for states would reduce this variability.
- Assessment has become the principal driver of most states' standards-based reform efforts. The result of this unintended development has been a reduced focus on the broader goals for instruction and learning that are at the heart of standards-based reform as it was originally envisioned.
- Some states have developed best practices and have built the necessary infrastructure to make them work. Other states can clearly benefit from those experiences.
- Past efforts to set standards, including contentious efforts in individual disciplines (e.g., U.S. history), more recent efforts (such as Achieve's focus on Algebra II for all), and the experience of states that have collaborated (e.g., the four New England states) offer valuable background for any plan to push for common K-12 standards.
- Defining rigor is straightforward if the focus is on the numbers of students who meet a particular proficiency standard at a fixed date, but if states shift their focus to students' development and learning over time, they will need to develop more flexible learning expectations.
- Policy makers and educators often have different perspectives on both the goals for reform and the effects of particular reforms in practice. Each group can learn from the other.
- There are significant practical obstacles to implementing common standards. Careful thought about options and ways to make such a transition, would be needed. For example, to what depth is uniformity necessary? By what process would common standards be developed, and who would be involved?
- Both teacher quality and focused textbook content are very significant factors that would not be directly addressed by more uniform standards. Without them, no real improvement is likely.

COSTS

- Although the estimated costs of standards-based reform and associated activities are higher than commonly recognized, they are still a minor fraction of education spending, especially relative to their importance.

- Addressing the many shortfalls in states' capacity to implement all of the elements of standards based reform would require increased spending.
- It would be useful to apply the cost framework (presented at the workshop) to additional states—particularly those that have come closest to establishing the infrastructure for systemic reform—to have some data on the costs for addressing the other components of reform.

QUESTIONS FOR THE NEXT WORKSHOP

- What would be necessary to develop a more uniform system of standards? That is, would it be necessary to develop a scholarly rationale for the structure of such a system? Is the research base on the ways in which student learning progresses sufficiently firm to support this effort? Alternatively, many advocate that standards be developed by mapping backward from conceptions of what students need to know to be ready for postsecondary study and careers. This idea raises the question of whether there is a consensus about what high school graduates need to have mastered.
- Many past efforts to develop standards have been significantly affected by political pressures in the states. How could a system based on common standards be structured so that it is relatively immune to such political pressures at the national level?
- What can be learned from international comparisons, particularly about countries that have had more success than the United States at producing high levels of achievement for all students, including those who are socioeconomically disadvantaged?

CONCLUDING THOUGHTS

The reports from the breakout sessions reinforced several common themes from the workshop. There seemed to be wide agreement that standards are now an accepted part of the educational landscape and that they play multiple roles in public education. Moreover, standards are seen as very important—and the need to improve them is seen as critical—because they are viewed as a means of achieving educational equity. However, neither the precise role that standards play nor their effects have been adequately documented.

One reason for the lack of clear answers about the effects of standards is that it is not completely clear that standards, and standards-based reform, have consistent definitions. It is clear that states' approaches to standards vary in many critical ways, not least in quality. Presenters and participants cited rigor, specificity, focus, and coherent learning progressions as critical aspects of high-quality standards, but there is no widely shared conception of quality or of the essential components of standards-based reform.

The variability in the implementation of standards-based reforms among states may reflect the lack of consensus about what good standards look like. Some noted, for example, that there is no obvious relationship between the coverage of content and performance on common measures, such as the National Assessment of Educational Progress. Others viewed the variation as an absolutely critical obstacle to the equality of opportunity that is a key goal of standards-based reform efforts. In some ways, assessments and proficiency scores have come to stand in for academic content standards, but few see this as a positive development. Many people believe that test-based accountability has made the goal of "proficiency" dwarf far more important education goals. Poor student outcomes should raise questions about the adequacy of curriculum, instruction, classroom materials, the structure of the school day and year, leadership, and other factors in education. Thus, for example, the goal of 100 percent proficiency by 2014 may be far less useful than establishing firm standards for states related to students' opportunity to learn.

Many participants shared the view that standards are a necessary, but not sufficient, component of systemic reform. The original theory of action was that if standards, assessments, and accountability systems were in place, everything else that needed to happen would follow. It seems clear now that this formulation was incomplete—that it left out two critical factors. First, it did not directly address teaching itself and the mechanisms through which teachers would adapt their instruction. Second, it did not address the need for political will to address the disparities in the educational opportunities offered to students in different settings by making the needed broader changes. The lack of will to push beyond the mechanics of standards documents and assessments and make fundamental changes in the way diverse students are served seems to be the reason that systemic reform has not been fully implemented in any state. Strategies for building on what has been accomplished through standards-based reform, such as a push for common standards, will need to take on those issues if they are to make a meaningful difference.

References

American Federation of Teachers. (2003). *Setting Strong Standards.* Washington, DC: American Federal of Teachers.

Carr, P. (2008). *Comparing State Proficiency Standards Using NAEP.* Presentation to the National Research Council Workshop on Assessing the Role of K-12 Academic Standards in States. Available: http://www7.nationalacademies.org/cfe/Carr%20Presentation.pdf [May 2008].

Center on Education Policy. (2007). *Answering the Question That Matters Most: Has Student Achievement Increased Since No Child Left Behind?* Washington, DC: Center on Education Policy.

Editorial Projects in Education. (2008). *Quality Counts.* Bethesda, MD: Editorial Projects in Education.

Goertz, M.E. (2007). *Standards-Based Reform: Lessons from the Past, Directions for the Future.* Paper presented at Clio at the Table: A Conference on the Uses of History to Inform and Improve Education Policy, Brown University.

Goertz, M.E. (2008). *Identifying the Costs of Standards-Based K-12 Education.* Presentation to the National Research Council Workshop on Assessing the Role of K-12 Academic Standards in States. Available: http://www7.nationalacademies.org/cfe/Goertz%20State%20Standards%20Presentation.pdf [April 2008].

Gross, P.R., Goodenough, U., Lerner, L.S., Haack, S., Schwartz, M., Schwartz, R., and Finn, C.E., Jr. (2005). *The State of State Science Standards.* Thomas B. Fordham Institute. Available: http://www.edexcellence.net/doc/Science%20Standards.FinalFinal.pdf [April 2008].

Harris, D., and Taylor, L. (2008a). Presentation to the National Research Council Workshop on Assessing the Role of K-12 Academic Standards in States. Available: http://www7.nationalacademies.org/cfe/1Harris%20and%20Taylor%20Presentation.pdf [April 2008].

Harris, D., and Taylor, L. (2008b). *The Resource Costs of Standards, Assessments, and Accountability.* Paper prepared for the National Research Council Workshop on Assessing the Role of K-12 Academic Standards in States. Available: http://www7.nationalacademies.org/cfe/Harris_Taylor%20State%20Standards%20Paper.pdf [April 2008].

Massell, D. (2008). *The Current Status and Role of Standards-Based Reform in the United States*. Paper prepared for the National Research Council Workshop on Assessing the Role of K-12 Academic Standards in States. Available: http://www7.nationalacademies.org/cfe/Massell%20State%20Standards%20Paper.pdf [May 2008].

National Center for Education Statistics. (2007). *Mapping 2005 State Proficiency Standards onto the NAEP Scales*. Research and Development Report. Available: http://nces.ed.gov/nationsreportcard/pubs/studies/2007482.asp [April 2008].

National Commission on Excellence in Education. (1983). *A Nation at Risk*. Washington, DC: National Commission on Excellence in Education.

Petrilli, M. (2007). Presentation to the National Research Council Workshop on Assessing the Role of K-12 Academic Standards in States. Available: http://www7.nationalacademies.org/cfe/Petrilli%20Presentation.pdf [April 2008].

Porter, A., Polikoff, M., and Smithson, J. (2008). *Is There a de Facto National Curriculum?: Evidence from State Standards*. Paper prepared for the National Research Council Workshop on Assessing the Role of K-12 Academic Standards in States. Available: http://www7.nationalacademies.org/cfe/Porter_Smithson%20State%20Standards%20Paper_Tables.pdf [May 2008].

Smith, M.S., and O'Day, J. (1991). Systemic school reform. In S.H. Fuhrman and B. Malen (Eds.), *The Politics of Curriculum and Testing*. (Yearbook of the Politics of Education Association). New York: Falmer Press.

Appendix

Workshop Agenda and Participants

Workshop on Assessing the Role of K-12 Academic Standards in States
January 17-18, 2008
National Academies Keck Center
500 Fifth Street, NW
Washington, DC
Room 100

AGENDA

Thursday, January 17, 2008

8:00 am **Continental Breakfast**

8:30 am **Introduction and Goals of Workshop Series**
Michael Feuer, NRC Division of Behavioral and Social Sciences and Education
Judith Rizzo, James B. Hunt, Jr. Institute for Educational Leadership and Policy
Lorraine McDonnell, University of California at Santa Barbara; Chair, Workshop Series Steering Committee

SESSION 1: SETTING THE STATE STANDARDS POLICY CONTEXT

Orienting the event's discussions in an analysis of existing literature and new research results on contemporary state standards-based reform efforts in California, Florida, Massachusetts, North Dakota, and Texas.

Framing Questions

1. What are the major roles that standards play in state K-12 education policy and practice?
2. What are the major strengths and weaknesses of K-12 state standards-based reform efforts with respect to achieving efficiency, equity, and quality? What are states doing to achieve these goals?

3. How and to what degree are the strengths and weaknesses of reform efforts related to the standards themselves? How and to what degree have the standards changed other education policies in states?
4. How and to what degree are the strengths and weaknesses of reform efforts related to having unique state standards?

9:00 am	**Introduction and Goals of Session** Lorraine McDonnell
9:15 am	**Roles, Impacts, and Perceptions of Standards: Review of Existing Research and Results from Elite Policymaker Interviews in California, Florida, Massachusetts, North Dakota, and Texas** Diane Massell, University of Michigan
9:45 am	**Moderated Discussion, Part 1: Research Perspectives** *Moderator* Lorraine McDonnell *Panelists* Lynn Olson, Education Week Brian Stecher, RAND Corporation
10:45 am	**Break**
11:00 am	**Moderated Discussion, Part 2: Policy and Practice Perspectives** *Moderator* Lorraine McDonnell *Panelists* Rae Ann Kelsch, North Dakota State Representative Scott Montgomery, Council of Chief State School Officers
12:00 pm	**Session 1 Central Themes** Lorraine McDonnell
12:15 pm	**Lunch**

SESSION 2: ESTIMATING COSTS TO STATES

Providing a framework for considering costs of state standards and accountability systems and applying that framework to developing empirical estimates in Florida, North Dakota, and Texas.

Framing Questions

1. What are the major activities states undertake to develop and maintain a standards-based K-12 education system? What is the nature of the costs to states associated with each of these major activities?
2. What are the sources of variation in these costs by state?
3. What are the costs associated with each major activity across select states?
4. How much do state cost estimates vary for each activity?
5. What are the conceptual and technical issues involved in developing empirical estimates of these costs?

1:15 pm **Introduction and Goals for Session**
Lauress (Laurie) Wise, HumRRO

1:30 pm **What States Do to Implement Standards-Based K-12 Education: Toward a Framework for Estimating State Costs**
Margaret (Peg) Goertz, University of Pennsylvania

1:50 pm **Developing Empirical Estimates of State Costs: Results from Florida, North Dakota, and Texas**
Douglas Harris, University of Wisconsin, Madison
Lori Taylor, Texas A&M University

2:30 pm **Break**

2:45 pm **Moderated Discussion, Part 1: Research and Business Perspectives**
Moderator
Laurie Wise

Panelists
Thomas Toch, Education Sector
Susan Traiman, Business Roundtable

3:30 pm **Break**

3:45 pm **Moderated Discussion, Part 2: Policy and Practice Perspectives**
Moderator
Laurie Wise

Panelists
David Driscoll, National Assessment Governing Board
R. Mark Harris, Human Capital Strategies

4:30 pm **Session 2 Central Themes**
Laurie Wise

4:45 pm **End of Formal Agenda for Day**

5:00 pm **Reception**
Keck Atrium

6:00 pm **Dinner**
Keck Atrium

Friday, January 18, 2008

8:00 am **Continental Breakfast**

SESSION 3: ANALYZING STATE STANDARDS

Assessing the similarities and differences across K-12 state content and performance standards in core academic subject areas.

Framing Questions

1. How and to what extent do K-12 state content standards vary in English/language arts, mathematics, and science at key grades?
2. How and to what extent do K-12 state performance standards vary in English/language arts, mathematics, and science at key grades?
3. How and to what extent does the implementation of K-12 state content and performance standards in classrooms vary in multiple academic subjects?

8:30 am **Introduction and Goals for Session**
Thomas Corcoran, Teachers College

8:45 am **Comparing State Content Standards: Topical Coverage and Cognitive Demand in Grades 4 and 8 Reading, Mathematics, and Science in Select States**
Andrew (Andy) Porter, University of Pennsylvania
John Smithson, University of Wisconsin

9:15 am **Comparing State Performance Standards: Results from Two Recent Studies**
Peggy G. Carr, National Center for Education Statistics
Michael Petrilli, Thomas B. Fordham Foundation

10:00 am **Moderated Discussion, Part 1: Research Perspectives**
Moderator
Tom Corcoran

Panelists
Barbara Reys, University of Missouri
William Schmidt, Michigan State University

10:45 am **Break**

11:00 am **Moderated Discussion, Part 2: Policy and Practice Perspectives**
Moderator
Tom Corcoran

Panelists
Peter McWalters, Rhode Island Commissioner of Education
Roy Romer, Strong American Schools Campaign

11:45 am **Session 3 Central Themes**
Tom Corcoran

BREAKOUT GROUPS: LOOKING ACROSS ISSUES

Developing ideas from across the three sessions in small, mixed-role groups.

12:00 pm **Working Lunch in Breakout Groups**
Goals, Introductions, Brainstorming

12:30 pm **Breakout Group Moderated Discussions**

1:45 pm **Reporting Out (Room 100)**
Group Moderators

2:15 pm **Wrap-Up of Workshop 1: Reflections on Workshop Themes**
Moderator
Lorraine McDonnell

Panelists
Robert Linn, University of Colorado
William Tate, Washington University in St. Louis
Karen Wixson, University of Michigan

3:00 pm **Looking Ahead to Workshop 2: Outstanding Issues and Questions**
Judith Rizzo

3:30 pm **Adjourn**

PARTICIPANTS

Allison Armour-Garb, Education Studies, Rockefeller Institute of Government
Alix Beatty, Center for Education, The National Academies
Ilene Berman, Education Division, National Governors Association Center for Best Practices
Peggy G. Carr, National Center for Education Statistics, U.S. Department of Education
Betty Carvellas, Teacher Advisory Council, The National Academies
Michael Casserly, Council of the Great City Schools
Thomas Corcoran, CPRE, Teachers College, Columbia University
Stephanie Dean, The Hunt Institute
David Driscoll, National Assessment Governing Board
Kelly Duncan, Center for Education, The National Academies
Stuart Elliott, Center for Education, The National Academies
Mark Emblidge, Virginia Board of Education
William Ewell, The Hunt Institute
Michael Feuer, Division of Behavioral and Social Sciences and Education, The National Academies
Catherine Freeman, Division of Behavioral and Social Sciences and Education, The National Academies
Michael Gilligan, The Hunt Institute
Margaret E. Goertz, Graduate School of Education, University of Pennsylvania
Steven Gorman, National Center for Education Statistics, U.S. Department of Education
Lisa Guckian, The Hunt Institute
Ferrel Guillory, The Hunt Institute
Daria Hall, The Education Trust
Douglas N. Harris, Educational Policy Studies, University of Wisconsin at Madison
R. Mark Harris, Human Capital Strategies, LLC
Margaret Hilton, Center for Education, The National Academies
Barbara Kapinus, National Education Association
Rae Ann Kelsch, North Dakota State Representative
Judy Koenig, Center for Education, The National Academies
Andrew Kolstad, National Center for Education Statistics, U.S. Department of Education
Barnett A. (Sandy) Kress, Akin Gump Stauss Hauer & Feld LLP
Stephanie Levin, CPRE, Graduate School of Education, University of Pennsylvania
Dane Linn, National Governors Association

Robert L. Linn, Department of Education, University of Colorado at Boulder
Bethany Little, Alliance for Excellent Education
Diane Massell, Consortium for Policy Research in Education, University of Michigan
Lorraine M. McDonnell, Department of Political Science, University of California at Santa Barbara
Gregory F. McGinity, The Broad Foundation
Peter McWalters, Rhode Island Department of Education
Talia Milgrom-Elcott, Carnegie Corporation
Scott Montgomery, Council of Chief State School Officers
Patricia Morison, Center for Education, The National Academies
Lynn Olson, *Education Week*
Michael Petrilli, Thomas B. Fordham Foundation
Morgan Polikoff, Policy, Management and Evaluation, University of Pennsylvania
Andy Porter, Graduate School of Education, University of Pennsylvania
Suellen Reed, Indiana Department of Education
Michael Resnick, National School Boards Association
Barbara J. Reys, Learning Teaching and Curriculum, University of Missouri
Judith Rizzo, The Hunt Institute
Roy Romer, Strong American Schools Campaign
Ian Rosenblum, Governor's Office of Pennsylvania
William Schmidt, Michigan State University
Sheila R. Schultz, Educational Policy Impact Center, Human Resources Research Organization
John Smithson, Measures of the Enacted Curriculum, University of Wisconsin at Madison
Brian Stecher, RAND Corporation
William Tate, Department of Arts and Sciences, Washington University in St. Louis
Lori Taylor, Bush School of Government, Texas A&M University
Thomas Toch, Education Sector
Lisa Towne, Center for Education, The National Academies
Susan Traiman, Education and Workforce Policy, Business Roundtable
Ruth Wattenberg, American Federation of Teachers
Lauress Wise, Human Resources Research Organization
Karen K. Wixson, School of Education, University of Michigan